DISCARDED
Goshen Public Library

GOSHEN PUBLIC LIBRARY
601 SOUTH FIFTH STREET
GOSHEN, IN 46526-3994

Child Abuse

Detecting Bias

Curriculum Consultant: JoAnne Buggey, Ph.D.
College of Education, University of Minnesota

By Stacey L. Tipp

OPPOSING JUNIORS VIEWPOINTS®

Greenhaven Press, Inc.
Post Office Box 289009
San Diego, CA 92198-0009

Titles in the opposing viewpoints juniors series:

Advertising	Male/Female Roles
AIDS	Nuclear Power
Alcohol	The Palestinian Conflict
Animal Rights	Patriotism
Causes of Crime	Population
Child Abuse	Poverty
Death Penalty	Prisons
Drugs and Sports	Smoking
Endangered Species	Television
The Environment	Toxic Wastes
Garbage	The U.S. Constitution
Gun Control	The War on Drugs
The Homeless	Working Mothers
Immigration	Zoos

Cover photo by: Third Coast Stock/© 1988 Ken Dufault

Library of Congress Cataloging-in-Publication Data

Tipp, Stacey L., 1963-
    Child abuse : detecting bias / by Stacey L. Tipp;
curriculum consultant, JoAnne Buggey.
       p. cm. — (Opposing viewpoints juniors)
    Summary: Presents opposing viewpoints on topics related to child abuse, accompanied by critical thinking activities to help the reader identify an author's bias.
    ISBN 0-89908-611-X
    1. Child abuse—United States—Juvenile literature. 2. Critical thinking—Juvenile literature. [1. Child abuse. 2. Critical thinking.] I. Buggey, JoAnne. II. Title. III. Series.
HV6626.5T56   1991
362.7'6—dc20   91-22101

No part of this book may be reproduced or used in any other form or by any other means, electrical, mechanical, or otherwise, including, but not limited to, photocopy, recording, or any information storage and retrieval system, without prior written permission from the publisher.

Copyright 1991 by Greenhaven Press, Inc.

CONTENTS

The Purpose of This Book: An Introduction to Opposing Viewpoints 4
Skill Introduction: Detecting Bias 5
Sample Viewpoint A: I think people who abuse their kids should not be allowed to keep them 6
Sample Viewpoint B: I think parents who have abused their kids should be given a second chance 7
Analyzing the Sample Viewpoints: Detecting Bias 8

Chapter 1
Preface: Should Child Abusers Be Imprisoned? 9
Viewpoint 1: Imprisoning abusers protects children 10
Viewpoint 2: Imprisoning abusers does not protect children 12
Critical Thinking Skill 1: Detecting Bias 14

Chapter 2
Preface: Should Children Be Allowed to Testify in Child Sexual Abuse Cases? 15
Viewpoint 3: Children make good witnesses 16
Viewpoint 4: Children do not make good witnesses 18
Critical Thinking Skill 2: Detecting Bias 20

Chapter 3
Preface: Does Foster Care Protect Abused Children? 21
Viewpoint 5: Foster care protects children from abuse 22
Viewpoint 6: Foster care does not protect children from abuse 24
Critical Thinking Skill 3: Detecting Bias in Editorial Cartoons 26

Chapter 4
Preface: Can School Prevention Programs Reduce Sexual Abuse of Children? 27
Viewpoint 7: School prevention programs can reduce child sexual abuse 28
Viewpoint 8: School prevention programs cannot reduce child sexual abuse 30
Critical Thinking Skill 4: Detecting Bias in Statements 32

THE PURPOSE OF THIS BOOK

An Introduction to Opposing Viewpoints

When people disagree, it is hard to figure out who is right. You may decide one person is right just because the person is your friend or relative. But this is not a very good reason to agree or disagree with someone. It is better if you try to understand why these people disagree. On what main points do they differ? Read or listen to each person's argument carefully. Separate the facts and opinions that each person presents. Finally, decide which argument best matches what you think. This process, examining an argument without emotion, is part of what critical thinking is all about.

This is not easy. Many things make it hard to understand and form opinions. People's values, ages, and experiences all influence the way they think. This is why learning to read and think critically is an invaluable skill.

Opposing Viewpoints Juniors books will help you learn and practice skills to improve your ability to read critically. By reading opposing views on an issue, you will become familiar with methods people use to attempt to convince you that their point of view is right. And you will learn to separate the authors' opinions from the facts they present.

Each Opposing Viewpoints Juniors book focuses on one critical thinking skill that will help you judge the views presented. Some of these skills are telling fact from opinion, recognizing propaganda techniques, and locating and analyzing the main idea. These skills will allow you to examine opposing viewpoints more easily. The viewpoints are placed in a running debate and are always placed with the pro view first.

SKILL INTRODUCTION

Detecting Bias

In this Opposing Viewpoints Juniors book, you will learn to detect bias.

All people are biased in favor of certain things and against others. For example, if you have favorite friends or relatives, it might be very hard for you to find fault with them, even when they do something obviously wrong or unkind. On the other hand, someone you particularly dislike might not be able to do anything right in your view. We do not always see things in an impartial, open-minded way. Our personal observations can be biased by what we like, dislike, or believe.

Similarly, authors of books, articles, and speeches are biased in favor of or against a particular point of view. Identifying an author's bias is an important critical thinking skill. Being able to detect the author's bias will help you determine whether the author is presenting an argument in a fair, objective manner or whether he or she is unfairly biased in favor of a particular view.

Many times bias, or point of view, is based on personal experience. For example, the owner of a corner convenience store often expresses her bad opinion of young people. She suggests that young people are thieves and are not being brought up right by their parents. She feels this way because she has caught young people stealing in her store. Although she has a reason for her bias, it is still a bias. Most of the young people she eyes with suspicion will not steal.

Sometimes bias is influenced by what parents or others in authority teach us. For example, members of the Ku Klux Klan believe blacks, Jews, and certain other minorities are inferior beings. They teach this bias to their children.

Sometimes bias is influenced by political events. For example, during World War II, the Japanese attacked an American military base. After this event, Japanese Americans were rounded up and sent to prison camps because officials feared they would act as spies against the United States. This decision was biased. Government officials treated all Japanese alike, even though many of them had lived in the United States and been loyal citizens for decades.

There are many other reasons people may be biased. In some cases, the reasons may seem like good ones. But biased statements must be carefully examined: Is the author's opinion based on objective information, or is it based on bias? How do you know? What reasons or evidence is used to support the statement? Do the reasons or evidence seem sound?

The authors of the viewpoints you will read in this book may be biased because of personal experience or for other reasons. Each author will try to persuade you that his or her opinion is correct. In order to figure out whether you will accept the author's opinion, you should attempt to discover whether the author is presenting the case fairly or with bias. Be aware of the author's point of view. What stand is he or she taking on the issue? Why would he or she take such a stand? Does the writer express fear, anger, or other strong feelings when describing his or her position? How do these emotions influence the objectivity of the viewpoint? Does the author use loaded words or phrases, that is, words that are overly positive or negative, to persuade you? Keep these questions in mind when analyzing the viewpoints in this book.

We asked two students to give their opinions on child abuse. Both students are biased. As you read, attempt to identify their biases.

SAMPLE VIEWPOINT A *Hannah:*

> **I think people who abuse their kids should not be allowed to keep them.**

Parents should never hit their kids. Those who do are bad parents. Violence is wrong, especially when it's used on someone who can't fight back, like a child. If a parent is ever found to have abused his or her kids, the government should take the kids away from the parents. Then the kids could get into a nice foster home or be adopted by people who won't abuse them.

If we leave kids with parents who abuse them, then the kids could get hurt even worse the next time. This happened to my friend Craig. Mr. Jones, Craig's dad, sometimes hits Craig really hard and a lot of the time Craig comes to school all black and blue. Our teacher saw the bruises one time so she told a social worker, a person who investigates child abuse cases. The social worker went to Craig's home to see what was going on. She decided Craig could continue to live with his dad for the time being. The social worker made a huge mistake though, because Craig's dad threw him down the stairs last week and broke his leg. If Craig had been put in foster care he wouldn't have a broken leg right now.

People who abuse their kids are evil and cruel. We should never let them abuse their children again.

SAMPLE VIEWPOINT B *Julius:*

> **I think parents who have abused their kids should be given a second chance.**

I don't think the government should take abused children away from their parents. Most parents who have abused their kids are not evil monsters. It's not that they don't love their kids. They really do. But it's not easy raising kids, and sometimes parents work so hard and get so tired that they just lash out in anger. All they need is to learn how to control their anger.

Anyway, you can't put all the kids who've been abused into foster homes because there's not enough room for them all. Foster care should be used only as a last resort in really serious abuse cases. The government should give most parents a second chance and help them become better parents.

My friend Sarah was put into foster care because she told her doctor that her mom hit her. Sarah's mom was really upset when she hit Sarah, because she and Sarah's dad had just divorced. Sarah was upset at her mom for hitting her, but she knows her mom loves her. Sarah really wants to go back home, but she's still in foster care and she hates it. Sarah's mom should be given a second chance to be a good parent.

Everybody makes mistakes. Children need their real parents, so we should try to keep families together.

ANALYZING THE SAMPLE VIEWPOINTS

Hannah and Julius have very different opinions about parents who abuse their children.

Hannah:

POINT OF VIEW (bias)

Parents who abuse their children are bad parents.

LOADED WORDS AND PHRASES USED TO SUPPORT HER VIEW

People who abuse their kids are *evil* and *cruel*; the social worker made a *huge mistake*.

PERSONAL EXPERIENCE THAT REINFORCES HER VIEW

Hannah's friend Craig's experience proves how bad parents can be and how they will keep abusing their kids until someone stops them.

CONCLUSIONS

Hannah is biased in favor of taking abused children away from their parents.

Julius:

POINT OF VIEW (bias)

Parents who abuse their children are not bad.

LOADED WORDS AND PHRASES USED TO SUPPORT HIS VIEW

Sarah *hates* foster care; *everybody makes mistakes*.

PERSONAL EXPERIENCE THAT REINFORCES HIS VIEW

Julius's friend Sarah's experience shows that parents who hit their kids are ordinary people experiencing stress and should be given a second chance.

CONCLUSIONS

Julius is biased in favor of keeping abused children and their parents together.

In this sample, Hannah and Julius both express bias when presenting their viewpoints. Based on this sample, who do you think is right about child abusers? How might your own bias affect your opinion?

CHAPTER 1

PREFACE: Should Child Abusers Be Imprisoned?

One of the most important questions in the child abuse debate is whether child abusers should be imprisoned for their crimes.

Many people believe child abusers should be imprisoned. They maintain that child abuse is a serious crime that deserves a severe punishment such as prison. Supporters of prison terms for abusers also believe this is the only way to ensure that the child victim will remain safe from his or her attacker. If abusers are not sent to prison, these observers believe, abused children cannot be sure that their attacker will not hurt them again.

Others disagree with this view. They argue that prison does not cure child abusers. It just keeps them off the streets for a while. These observers say that child abusers should be treated for their problems rather than imprisoned. They believe that only psychological counseling and medical treatment can really help abusers stop hurting children.

A critical thinker examining a viewpoint on this issue should be careful to look for the author's bias. An author may be strongly biased in favor of or against the imprisonment of child abusers. Watch for bias as you read the next two viewpoints.

VIEWPOINT 1   Imprisoning abusers protects children

> **Editor's Note:** In the following viewpoint, the author argues that child abusers should be imprisoned. She believes that only this action can protect children from abuse. Follow the questions in the margin. They will help you identify the author's bias.

In this first paragraph you can already identify the author's bias. Words and phrases such as "lock child abusers up and throw away the key" reveal the author's bias.

The abuse of young children is the most horrible crime in the whole world. People who do this are criminals and should be treated as criminals. Judges should lock child abusers up and throw away the key. Only by taking strong action can the judges make certain that abusers never again hurt young children.

Unless something is done to stop these criminals, the number of abuse victims will rise. It is scary how many children are abused in this country. Some studies say that two million American children are physically or sexually abused each year.

The criminal justice system does not take the crime of child abuse seriously enough. Too many child abusers receive very light punishment or no punishment at all. This is really unfair. A child can suffer terrible physical and emotional damage at the hands of the abuser. Sometimes a child's whole life is ruined.

"A slap on the wrist" is a loaded phrase. It suggests that justice was not done in this case.

All too often, child abusers get off with a slap on the wrist. In one case, a five-year-old girl was raped by a neighbor. The girl was terrified after the attack and had continued nightmares. The

Fear of her abuser is shown in this self-portrait by a 7-year-old.
Used with permission of Greenwich House Children's Safety Project, New York.

10   JUNIORS

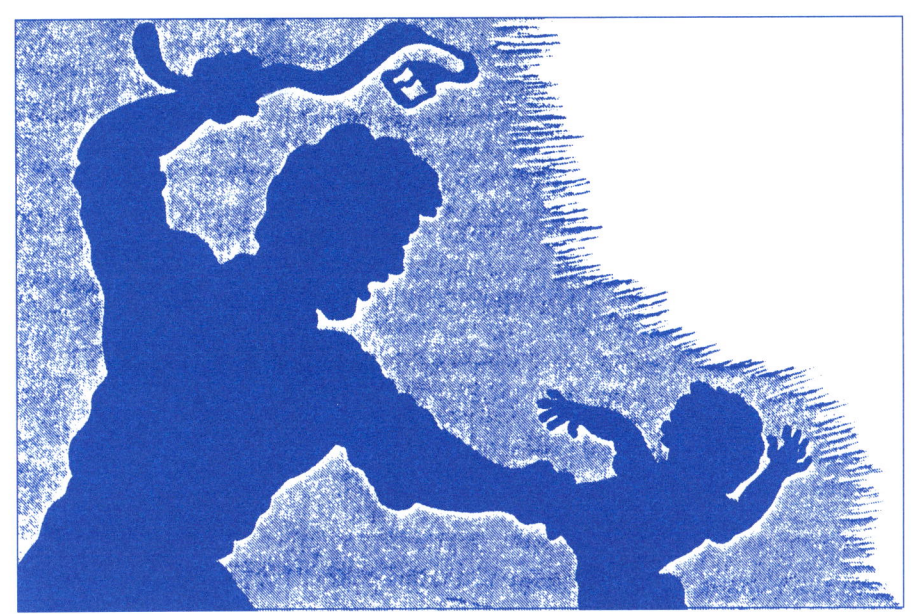

CHILD ABUSE ON THE RISE
© Alexander/Rothco. Reprinted with permission.

neighbor did not suffer one little bit. His only punishment was to go see a psychiatrist once a week for six months. His victim, on the other hand, will be seeing a psychiatrist for years.

Far too many people look upon the child abuser as a sick person who needs help and counseling. They could not be more wrong. Child abuse is a violent crime and child abusers should be locked up like other violent criminals. The people who advocate treatment rather than prison do not care about the rights of children. They only care about the rights of abusers. It is time abused children had someone to speak up for them.

If society is serious about protecting children from physical and sexual abuse, it must send a strong message to child abusers. These offenders must learn that if they hurt children they will have to pay a very big price: They will lose their freedom and be locked away in prison where they belong.

> The author is biased against those who advocate treatment rather than prison terms for child abusers. Loaded phrases like "they could not be more wrong," and "they only care about the rights of abusers" reveal the author's bias.

> The main idea of this paragraph is that child abusers must pay for their crimes. The author is biased in favor of imprisonment.

Should abusers be imprisoned?

The author assumes that imprisonment will protect children from abuse and punish abusers. Does the author express any emotion such as fear or anger when presenting her view? If so, how did that feeling influence her opinion?

CHILD ABUSE **11**

VIEWPOINT 2: Imprisoning abusers does not protect children

Editor's Note: In the following viewpoint, the author argues that imprisoning abusers will do nothing to protect children from abuse. She maintains that putting abusers in prison may even harm children. Watch for examples of bias in the author's argument.

> **The author could make this paragraph less biased by not calling advocates of prison terms for child abusers "cruel." Most people who recommend prison terms for abusers want to protect children and ensure that child abusers receive a suitable punishment.**

Putting child abusers in prison will do nothing to protect children. People who recommend putting these abusers in prison are just plain cruel. They ignore the fact that most abusers are victims, too. For example, studies show that somewhere between 33 percent and 80 percent of abusers were abused as children. If society imprisons abusers, it only hurts these victims more. Child abusers need help and compassion, not hatred.

Society has a duty to protect children from abuse, but imprisonment is not the solution. The only real solution is to provide child abusers with medical treatment and psychological counseling. Treatment can help child abusers understand what makes them abuse children and how they can change their behavior. While prison will help keep the abuser locked up for a while, it will do nothing to cure him or her or protect children.

> **Do you agree that abused children may feel guilty or sad if their abusers are sent to prison? What other emotions might they feel?**

Another problem with imprisonment is that it often hurts the child to see the abuser go to prison. The vast majority of child abusers are either family members or acquaintances of the abused child. Imprisoning the abuser is likely to take away someone the child

Joel Pett/*Lexington Herald-Leader*. Reprinted with permission.

12   JUNIORS

Reported Cases of Child Abuse

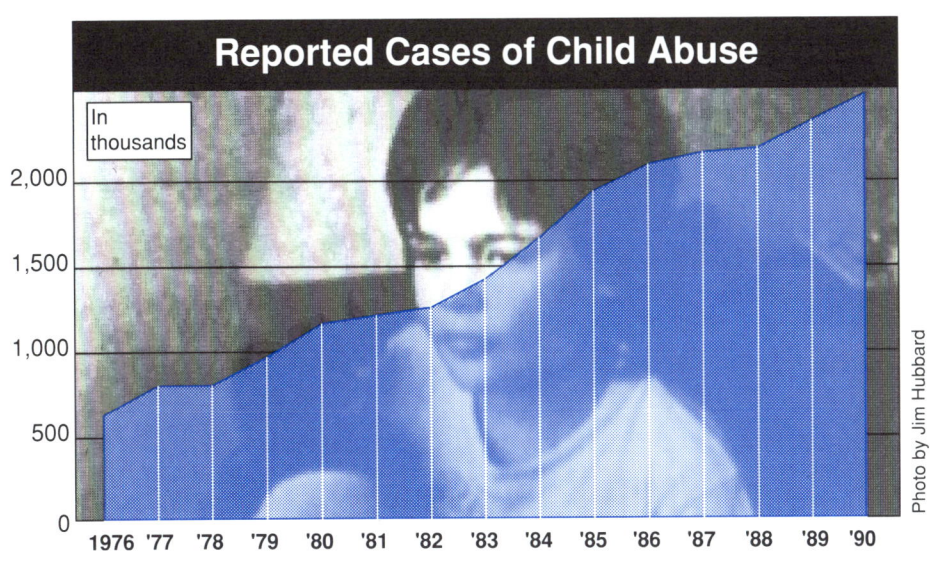

Sources: American Humane Assn.; National Committee for the Prevention of Child Abuse. Adapted from Patricia Mitchell/*Los Angeles Times*.

Photo by Jim Hubbard

loves. The child may feel guilty and sad if the abuser is put in prison. In fact, some studies show that the pain the child feels when the abuser is imprisoned is sometimes as bad as the abuse itself. We should try to heal families, not split them up. Imprisonment is a cruel and useless strategy.

Another problem is that the abuser can use the threat of his or her own imprisonment to keep the child from telling on the abuser. For example, if Bob is abusing his six-year-old son Mark, he may say, "Mark, if you tell, Daddy will be sent to prison and you will never see me again." Mark may really love his dad despite the abuse and will not tell because he is afraid Bob will go to prison. If Mark knew that his dad would get treatment and not prison, he might tell his teacher or some other adult about the abuse.

Putting abusers in prison does not protect children and does not cure the abuser of his or her problem. People who abuse children are not criminals, they are sick. They should be treated by doctors, not prison guards. People who want child abusers to be put in prison are spiteful. They will not face the fact that most abusers, like the kids they abuse, are victims. They deserve help not punishment.

> Do you agree with the author that Mark would be more likely to tell on his father if he knew Bob would get treatment, not jail?

> Do you think the author's opinion of child abusers is objective (fair)? Why or why not?

Should abusers receive treatment instead of prison?

Why does the author believe abusers should be sent to treatment programs rather than prison? What are some of the "loaded" terms the author uses to establish her views? How do these loaded terms reveal her bias?

CHILD ABUSE 13

CRITICAL THINKING SKILL 1
Detecting Bias

After reading the two viewpoints on whether child abusers should be imprisoned, make a chart similar to the one made for Hannah and Julius on page 8. First, state each author's point of view. Next, list any loaded words or phrases used to support his or her view. Then write down any examples of personal experiences (either the author's own personal experience or the personal experience of the people quoted) that might bias his or her view. Finally, state your conclusion about the authors' biases. A chart is started for you below.

Viewpoint 1:

POINT OF VIEW

LOADED WORDS AND PHRASES USED TO SUPPORT HER VIEW

"the most horrible crime in the whole world," "a slap on the wrist"

PERSONAL EXPERIENCE THAT REINFORCES HER VIEW

CONCLUSIONS

Viewpoint 2:

POINT OF VIEW

LOADED WORDS AND PHRASES USED TO SUPPORT HER VIEW

"a cruel and useless strategy"

PERSONAL EXPERIENCE THAT REINFORCES HER VIEW

CONCLUSIONS

After completing your chart, answer the following questions:

1. How do you think the authors could have made their arguments more objective, less biased?

2. Even after recognizing the authors' biases, which argument did you find most convincing? Why?

14   JUNIORS

CHAPTER 2

PREFACE: Should Children Be Allowed to Testify in Child Sexual Abuse Cases?

A major disagreement in the child abuse debate concerns whether sexually abused children can be effective witnesses in the trials of their abusers.

Many people believe children can make good witnesses. These people maintain that children know how to tell the truth. They say that children know the difference between right and wrong and can distinguish between fantasy and reality. They also point to studies which show that children's charges of sexual abuse are rarely proven false. These observers argue that abused children talk about their abuse in such detail that it is impossible for them to have made it up.

Others maintain that children are known to make up stories of sexual abuse. They may be coached by adults who hold a grudge against the accused person. They also may be encouraged by over-enthusiastic physicians and social workers who are anxious to prove that abuse occurred. These critics agree that child sexual abuse is a very serious problem. However, they question whether a child's word is reliable enough to be the basis of the conviction of an adult. These critics argue that child abuse investigators must try to find evidence that supports the child's statements and not rely solely on the child's word.

As you read the next two viewpoints, look for bias in the authors' views.

VIEWPOINT 3 Children make good witnesses

> **Editor's Note:** In the following viewpoint, the author argues that children can make good witnesses in child sexual abuse cases. She believes the testimony of the child victim is often necessary to put the abuser in prison. Look for examples of bias in the author's argument.

Can you find the loaded terms in this paragraph? How do they reveal the author's point of view?

Children can make very good witnesses in child sexual abuse cases. After all, they are the victims of the abuse and they should be allowed to testify. Many people do not think children make good witnesses. These people are very wrong. Children are willing and able to tell the truth.

People who say children do not make good witnesses argue that youngsters often make up stories about abuse. However, studies show that it is rare for children to do this. Some experts say that more than ninety-nine times out of one hundred, charges of sexual abuse made by children are true. While children do fantasize and make things up, they do not fantasize about having sexual relations with adults. Besides, children who have been sexually abused are able to describe their abuse in such detail that they could not have made it all up.

Courtroom trauma

© 1989 *USA Today*. Reprinted with permission.

Unfortunately, courts often do not believe children tell the truth or are able to tell the difference between what is real and what is made up. This attitude is a disgrace. Many adults get up on the witness stand and lie. But courts do not assume that adults will lie as they assume children will.

The reason some children do not make good witnesses is that they are scared about having to appear in court. After all, imagine if you had to sit in the witness box and answer questions from lawyers and the judge while your abuser is sitting right there watching you. It is not that children cannot tell the truth or that they make bad witnesses, but they are often so frightened in the courtroom they are unable to get the words out. Fortunately, some courts are trying to help young witnesses testify. For example, in many cases abused children are allowed to answer questions in a quiet place away from the courtroom. The child's answers are recorded on a videotape which is later played in court without the child having to be present.

People who say abused children do not make good witnesses do not care about the children. They only care about the abuser. Children do make good witnesses when the courtroom experience is made less scary for them. If children are not allowed to testify, more and more abusers will go free. This is because in many cases the abused child is the only person with the evidence needed to put the abuser in prison. If the courts ignore what abused children have to say, their abusers will just go back out into society and hurt more innocent children.

What emotion is the author expressing here?

Do you agree that courts must do more to help young witnesses testify? Why or why not?

The author could have made this argument more objective, less biased, by not attacking people who say children do not make good witnesses. Most of these people *do* care about children. But they worry that innocent people might be harmed if falsely accused by child witnesses.

Can children make good witnesses?

What is the author's point of view? Find five words that are used to help persuade the reader to accept the author's point of view.

CHILD ABUSE **17**

VIEWPOINT 4 Children do not make good witnesses

Editor's Note: The author of the following viewpoint does not believe that children make good witnesses in sexual abuse cases. He believes children often lie about being abused.

What is the author's opinion of child witnesses? How do you know it is biased?

What loaded words and phrases are used in this paragraph?

Children make very bad witnesses in child sex abuse cases. They often make up stories about being abused and they repeat their lies on the witness stand. Child sex abuse is a serious problem. But it is a fact that children tell lies about abuse all the time. Sometimes they cannot even tell the difference between what is true and what they have made up.

Many cases prove children make up accusations of sexual abuse. For example, take the case of the Virginia McMartin Preschool in Manhattan Beach, California. In this case, Ray Buckey, the grandson of the school's founder, his mother, and several other teachers were accused of abusing the children in their care. The children said they had seen devil worship in a church, had been taken to graveyards where they had dug up dead bodies, had been buried alive, and had seen Ray Buckey kill a horse with a baseball bat! These stories are ridiculous. The jury thought so, too. Charges were dropped against most of the accused teachers. In January 1990, Ray Buckey and his mother were quite rightly found not guilty of fifty-two counts of child abuse.

Many children who tell tales about child abuse are coached into saying these things by an adult who bears a grudge against the accused person. This often happens in child custody cases where parents are fighting over who their child will live with. For example, a mother may coach her child to say that the child's daddy abused her. The mother hopes the court will give her full custody of the child. Studies show how easy it is to pressure a child into lying about abuse. In 1986, for example, sixteen hundred charges of sexual abuse were made in child custody disputes. About 60 percent of these charges were found to be lies.

Sometimes children make up stories to punish their parents for making them do things they do not want to do—like going to school or doing chores. In New York, a seven-year-old boy named Michael told his teachers that a bruise on his back came from a beating his father had given him. That evening, Michael and his four brothers and sisters were taken from their home and put in foster care. Investigators later discovered that Michael had made the whole story up because his father told him he had to go to school.

FORMS OF CHILD ABUSE

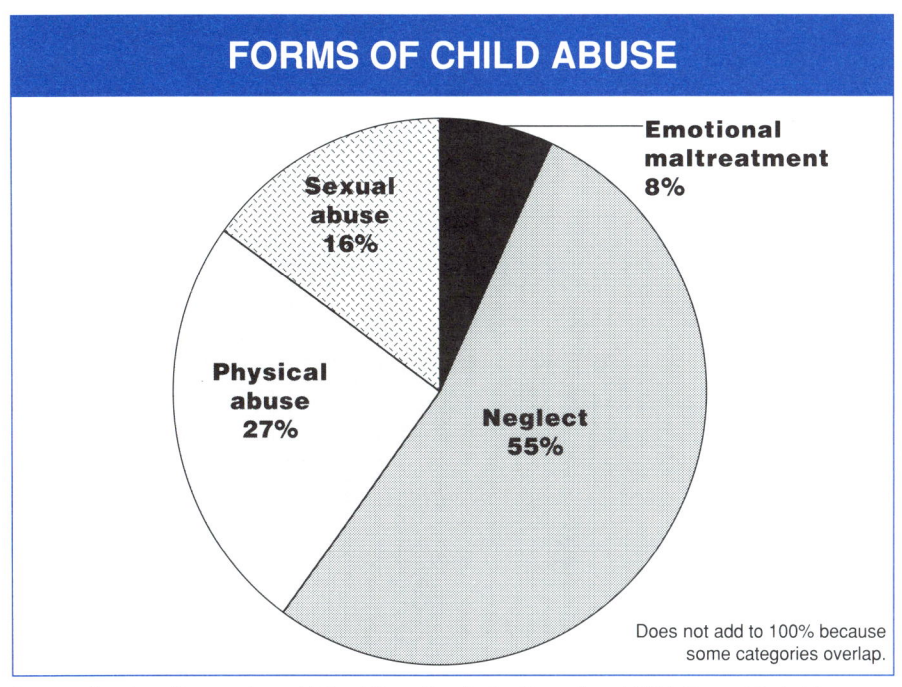

- Emotional maltreatment 8%
- Sexual abuse 16%
- Physical abuse 27%
- Neglect 55%

Does not add to 100% because some categories overlap.

Sources: American Humane Assn.; National Committee for the Prevention of Child Abuse. Adapted from Patricia Mitchell/*Los Angeles Times*.

Because children are known to lie about being abused, investigators must really look into child abuse cases to find out the truth. If they fail to do this, many innocent people could be sent to prison for something they did not do.

Does the evidence presented in this and the previous paragraph convince you that children often lie about child abuse? Why or why not?

Should children be allowed to testify?

The author does not believe that children make good witnesses. List two loaded phrases he uses that reveal his bias against child witnesses.

CHILD ABUSE   19

CRITICAL THINKING SKILL 2
Detecting Bias

This activity will allow you to practice identifying bias. The paragraphs below focus on the subject matter of this book. Read each paragraph and consider it carefully, deciding whether or not the author is biased. Read the statement following the paragraph and select the best answer to complete it.

If you are doing this activity as a member of a class or group, compare your answers with other people's. You may find that some have different answers than you do. Listening to the reasons others give for their responses can help you in identifying bias.

EXAMPLE: Many people think that child abuse is one of the most serious problems facing America today. Some experts believe that about two hundred thousand children are sexually or physically abused each year. Others believe the figure is closer to two million.

The author of this paragraph
a. reveals a dislike for child abusers.
b. takes no sides.
c. does not believe child abuse is a problem.

ANSWER: b. The author shows no particular bias toward any side.

1. People who sexually or physically abuse children must be harshly punished. Child abuse is a serious crime and deserves a severe punishment such as prison. The experience of abuse can completely destroy an innocent child's life. Years after the abuse has ended, the damage remains.

The author of this paragraph
a. shows sympathy for child abusers.
b. tries to remain objective.
c. shows sympathy for child abuse victims.

2. Many prisons have no available treatment programs to help convicted child abusers overcome their problems. Prisons just keep offenders locked up but do not cure them. Because most child abusers were themselves the helpless victims of abusers, we should not send them to prison for punishment. Instead, we should send them to treatment programs for help.

The author of this paragraph expresses a bias against prisons and in favor of using treatment programs to help child abusers. Which of the words and phrases used in the paragraph best shows the author's bias?
a. no available treatment programs.
b. helpless victims of abusers.
c. send them to treatment programs for help.

3. Studies show that many people who were abused as children become abusers when they grow up. Some studies estimate that one-third of abused children become abusers. However, other studies estimate the figure to be as high as 85 percent.

The author of this paragraph
a. is sympathetic to child abusers.
b. is sympathetic to child abuse victims.
c. takes no sides.

CHAPTER 3

PREFACE: Does Foster Care Protect Abused Children?

Each year, many thousands of abused children are removed from their homes and placed in foster care to protect them from further abuse. Ideally, a child is placed in a foster home on a temporary basis while social workers try to sort out the family's problems. While some children may eventually be returned to their own homes, others stay in foster care for many years. Some foster children are adopted, either by their foster parents or by other people.

Many people strongly support foster care, believing it can protect children from violent and abusive parents. The National Foster Parent Association explains how foster homes can also help children realize that not all adults are abusive: "After spending time [in a foster home], children learn for the first time that they're hit and abused not because they're horrible and worthless children, but because of a madness in their home. They'll learn that a house can be different—that there are adults to trust and rely on who will never beat you or blame you, but comfort you instead."

Others do not share this favorable view of foster care. Critics believe foster care harms children. They maintain that many foster parents are abusive, and that social workers do not properly monitor the care of foster children. As a result, they say, many foster children suffer worse abuse and neglect than they did in their own homes. Critics of foster care can cite many horrific examples of children who were abused in foster care. One case they tell about is a foster child who was so neglected that he weighed only seventeen pounds at age nine.

As you can tell from the above arguments, each side holds a strong bias about foster care. See if you can detect it in the next two viewpoints.

VIEWPOINT 5 Foster care protects children from abuse

Editor's Note: The author of the following viewpoint strongly supports foster care. He believes foster care can protect abused children from further abuse. Look for examples of bias in his argument.

What are the loaded words and phrases used in this paragraph? How do they reveal the author's bias?

Foster homes can help children who have been abused or neglected by their natural parents. There are about two hundred thousand foster families in America, and they are a safe refuge for abused children. Foster parents are loving, caring, unselfish people. They willingly open their homes and their hearts to children who have suffered abuse. America owes them a big thanks.

The Child Welfare League of America says there were about 340,000 kids in foster care in 1991. By 1995, they expect there will be 500,000. The growing number of children in foster care is partly due to rising drug and alcohol abuse among parents. When parents who are on drugs begin abusing and neglecting their kids, foster care can step in and protect the children. Of course, many parents neglect and abuse their kids without being on drugs. These parents are just cruel.

Kids are safe in foster homes, but often they are returned to their natural parents who resume abusing them. Social workers who care more about the rights of the parents than the rights of

The author expresses anger at social workers and the natural parents of foster children. Strong emotions often reveal bias. In this case, the bias is that most natural parents do not deserve to get their children back from foster care.

© Adair/Rothco. Reprinted with permission.

22 JUNIORS

children are often to blame. JoAnn and Jim Miller of Elkhart, Indiana, have given homes to about fifty foster children. They know all too well the dangers of returning children to abusive parents. A social worker insisted that one of their foster children, a thirteen-year-old girl named Tammy, be returned to her parents. When Tammy got home, her stepfather sexually abused her.

The natural parents of some of the Millers' other foster kids have also shown how little they care for their children. One of the Millers' foster kids waited for hours for his father to pick him up for a visit. Finally, the boy fell asleep with his chin on the windowsill. This neglectful father did not bother to show up until three days later. Another of their foster kids refused to turn five because his mom did not give him a birthday party. JoAnn Miller eventually had to give the mother a cake mix so the little boy could celebrate his birthday.

Foster parents like the Millers are caring people who do a great deal to help abused children. Many of the natural parents of the children in foster care are cruel and selfish. They have no right to get their kids back. While a few parents do work hard to change and perhaps do deserve another chance, they are a very small minority. As Patrick Murphy, the Public Guardian for Chicago's twenty-four thousand neglected and abused children, puts it, "We send kids home to coke-addicted moms and their sexually abusive boyfriends. . . . Some of these parents just don't deserve their kids."

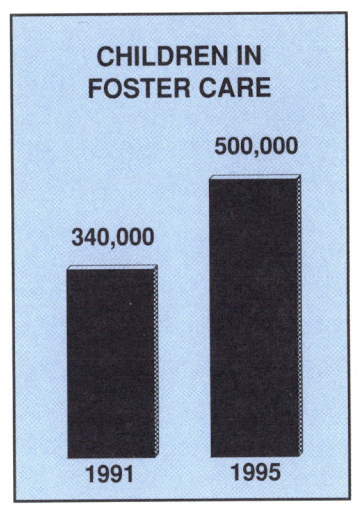

CHILDREN IN FOSTER CARE

500,000

340,000

1991   1995

Source: Child Welfare League of America

How might the author make this paragraph more objective, less biased?

Can foster care protect children from abuse?

The author believes foster care is necessary to protect abused children. Do you think he makes a good case for foster care? Why or why not?

CHILD ABUSE   **23**

VIEWPOINT 6: Foster care does not protect children from abuse

Editor's Note: In the following viewpoint, the author argues that foster care harms rather than protects children. Watch for words and phrases that may indicate bias.

What emotion is the author expressing here?

Does the evidence presented in this and the previous paragraph convince you that foster care harms children? Why or why not?

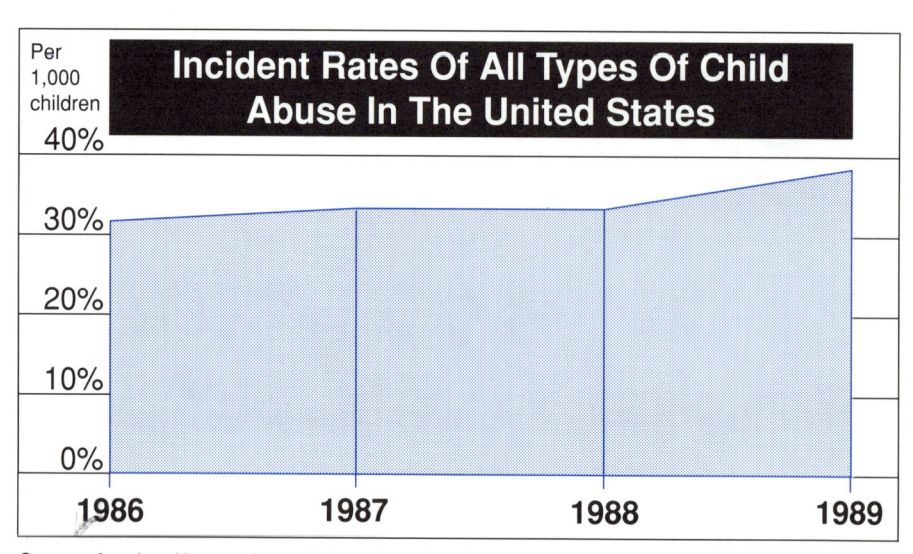

It is a fact that abused children are more likely to be harmed than helped by foster care. While many foster parents are nice, caring people, others are cruel and abusive. Sometimes children are removed from their own homes only to suffer worse abuse in a foster home. The foster care system is a national disgrace. If something is not done soon about abuse in foster homes, the effects on America's children will be terrible.

An example will prove this point beyond any doubt. In this case, a one-year-old girl was placed in a foster home. The girl suffered from epilepsy, a disorder of the brain, and needed to see a doctor regularly for her condition. However, her uncaring foster parents did not take her to her doctor's appointments. After two-and-a-half years and a lot of pressure from the girl's doctor, the child was removed from the foster home. What did the social workers do next? They continued to use this foster home for the care of other abused children. The social workers in this case should be fired.

Studies show that children in foster homes are more likely to be abused than children living with their natural parents. In 1986, the National Foster Care Education Project did a nationwide survey of abuse in foster families. The survey showed rates of abuse were sometimes more than ten times higher for foster children than for

Incident Rates Of All Types Of Child Abuse In The United States

Per 1,000 children

Year	Rate
1986	~30%
1987	~30%
1988	~30%
1989	~35%

Sources: American Humane Assn.; National Committee for the Prevention of Child Abuse

children living in their own homes.

There are many reasons why children in foster homes may suffer worse abuse than kids living in their own homes. One is that social workers have too many kids to keep an eye on, so they cannot protect every foster child from abuse. Another is that there are not enough good foster homes to go round. So social workers end up using foster homes they know are no good. A final reason is that foster parents and their foster children are strangers to each other. There are no blood relationships or family ties which can prevent serious abuse from occurring.

The foster care system in this country is a disgrace. America's children deserve better. Instead of breaking up families, social workers should try to keep families together. If they helped families work out their problems and got abusive parents the treatment they need, many kids would not end up being abused in foster care.

Do you find any of these reasons convincing? Why or why not?

How good is foster care?

How does the author attempt to persuade you that foster care harms children? Do you think her argument is convincing? Why or why not?

CRITICAL THINKING SKILL 3

Detecting Bias in Editorial Cartoons

Throughout this book, you have seen cartoons that illustrate the ideas in the viewpoints. Editorial cartoons are an effective and usually humorous way of presenting an opinion on an issue. Cartoonists, like writers, can be biased in presenting their opinions. In this activity, you will be asked to detect the bias in the cartoon pictured below.

© Canton/Rothco. Reprinted with permission.

1. What opinion do you think the cartoonist has of child abuse?
2. Why do you think the cartoonist uses a rag doll to illustrate the effects of child abuse?
3. What other elements in the cartoon reveal the cartoonist's bias?
4. For further practice, look at the editorial cartoons featured in the daily newspaper. Try to identify the biases in the cartoons.

CHAPTER 4

PREFACE: **Can School Prevention Programs Reduce Sexual Abuse of Children?**

In recent years, many schools have started child abuse prevention classes. These classes try to give children the knowledge and skills they need to avoid sexual abuse by strangers and family members. For example, programs try to teach children the difference between good and bad touching. They also tell children where to go for help if someone tries to abuse them.

Many people strongly support these programs. They like these programs for two main reasons. First, they believe child abusers are less likely to abuse children who have been taught how to avoid abuse. Second, they believe that many abused children will be more likely to tell on their abusers if sexual abuse is discussed in school.

Other people do not agree that school prevention programs can reduce child abuse. Critics believe that these programs actually do more harm than good. They say many children may be confused or frightened by the materials presented in the programs. Because of their fears, some children may avoid even normal touching from their parents and other loved ones.

The next two viewpoints examine school prevention programs. Be sure to watch for bias in the authors' views.

VIEWPOINT 7 — School prevention programs can reduce child sexual abuse

Editor's Note: The author of the following viewpoint argues that school prevention programs can reduce sexual abuse of children. He believes all schools should have these programs. Watch for words and phrases that may indicate bias.

Is the author's opinion of sex abuse prevention programs objective? How can you tell?

Sexual abuse is one of the worst things that can happen to young children. To help prevent this abuse, many schools are starting programs to educate kids about child abuse. They teach children how to recognize abuse, how to say no to abuse, and how to get help. These programs are great. Every school in America should have programs like these!

There are many good reasons why parents should support these programs. One is that experts are learning more and more about the terrible ways sexual abuse affects children. Abused children often suffer from nightmares, bedwetting, anxiety, aggression, and many other severe behavioral problems. Unfortunately, these problems can continue into adulthood. Adults who were sexually abused as children often find it hard to enjoy trusting and caring personal relationships. Many of them become abusers themselves. Society has a duty to educate children about child abuse, because education is one of the best ways to protect children from becoming victims.

COPING WITH SEXUAL ABUSE

- There is a difference between good and bad touching.
- You can control who touches your body and where you are touched.
- Tell someone you trust if you experience bad touching.
- Never keep secrets about bad touching.
- You can say "no" and defend yourself against bad touching.
- There are people to help you if you have been abused.

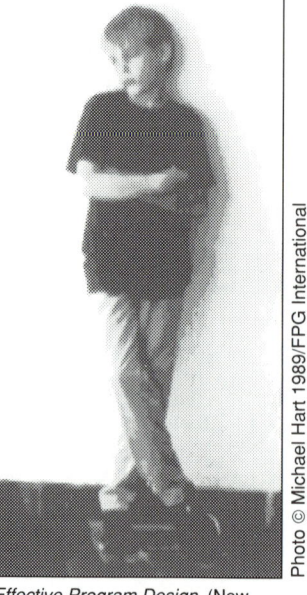

Text adapted from Deborah Daro, *Confronting Child Abuse: Research for Effective Program Design.* (New York: The Free Press, 1988).

A second reason to expand these programs is that they work! Studies show that kids who have been taught about sexual abuse in school have more knowledge about how to avoid abuse than do children who have not been taught about it. They are also more aware about where to go for help if they have been abused.

Researchers have interviewed many convicted child abusers. These abusers say they steer clear of children who are likely to tell about the abuse. Child abusers typically attack lonely and isolated children. These children must learn the protective skills taught in school-based prevention programs.

A final reason for having these programs in schools is that many kids already tell their teachers about abuse. They do this because they like and trust their teachers. Imagine how many more kids might come forward if they had already discussed abuse in the classroom. School-based programs are a great opportunity for abused kids to speak up.

> Do you agree that abused children will be more likely to talk about their abuse in schools with prevention programs?

Education is one of the great weapons in the fight against the terrible evil of sexual abuse. If society does not use the schools to fight sexual abuse, it will almost certainly lose the war against this sickness.

> How might the author make this paragraph more objective, less biased?

> **Do school prevention programs work?**
>
> The author believes school-based programs help prevent the sexual abuse of children. Do you find his argument convincing? Why or why not?

VIEWPOINT 8 | School prevention programs cannot reduce child sexual abuse

Editor's Note: The author of the following viewpoint does not believe school prevention programs can reduce child sexual abuse. Instead, the author argues these programs merely confuse and frighten children.

What words does the author use to persuade you to agree with his point of view?

School-based programs that try to help children avoid sexual abuse are a disgraceful waste of money. They are also dangerous because they frighten and confuse children. These programs should be taken out of the schools immediately.

One problem is that these programs are often directed toward very young children. These children, who have had no experience of sexual abuse, may have difficulty understanding the issue. Even if they understand the information, they may not be able to use it successfully if confronted by a sex abuser. Also, because young children cannot retain information for very long, they may quickly forget what they have been taught about sexual abuse.

School-based prevention programs can confuse children about good and bad touching. For example, after learning about sexual abuse, children may interpret an innocent touch from a parent or a teacher as sexual abuse. Children may also become fearful that they will be abused by their parents. One study found that after

© Graston/Rothco. Reprinted with permission.

30 JUNIORS

seeing a play about sexual abuse, 93 percent of a group of children thought that sexual assault could happen in their family.

Another drawback to these programs is that people children should be able to trust, like parents and teachers, may be afraid to touch their children. They may fear the child will interpret their action as sexual abuse. This is the reason one Chicago school superintendent told his teachers not to touch their students in any manner. This is truly sad, because young children need the benefits of healthy touch to thrive and grow.

The sexual abuse of young children is a very serious problem. However, most children will never experience sexual abuse. It seems unwise, therefore, to confuse and frighten so many students about something that will never affect them. The best thing to do is to get rid of these programs before they damage even more children.

> Do you agree with the author that it might be better to get rid of these programs if they are frightening children?

> How valuable are school-based prevention programs?
>
> Have you ever participated in one of these programs? If so, did you find the experience good or bad? Why?

CHILD ABUSE 31

CRITICAL THINKING SKILL 4
Detecting Bias in Statements

This activity will allow you to practice detecting bias. The statements below focus on the subject matter of this book. Read each statement and consider it carefully. *Mark B for any statement that you believe is biased. Mark N for any statement you believe is not biased. Mark U for any statement for which you are uncertain.* Be sure to provide a reason for your answer.

If you are doing this activity as a member of a class or group, compare your answers with those of other class or group members. Discussing your answer with others may give you a new perspective on your own biases.

EXAMPLE: The only place to put convicted child abusers is in prison. They are a threat to children and should pay for their crimes. Prison is the only suitable punishment for these animals.

ANSWER: B, bias. The author does not make his case in an objective manner. He does not say why prison is the only place to put child abusers. He also calls them "animals," which is clearly a loaded word.

1. Child sex abuse prevention programs in schools are a waste of money. They frighten children and make them afraid to be touched by their parents and other loved ones.

   Answer _____ Reason _____
   _____

2. The foster care system in this country is a disgrace. The system was set up to help children, but it actually hurts them. We must do something quickly to rescue children from cruel and abusive foster parents. Foster care should only be used as a very, very last resort.

   Answer _____ Reason _____
   _____

3. Many schools have introduced programs that teach children how to avoid sexual abuse. While many people support these programs, others fear that they may frighten and confuse children.

   Answer _____ Reason _____
   _____

4. Child abusers deserve our sympathy and compassion. Many of them were abused as children. Society should provide these abusers with the treatment and counseling programs they need to overcome their problems.

   Answer _____ Reason _____
   _____

DISCARDED
Goshen Public Library

J 362.76 TIP — Tipp, Stacey L., Child abuse

W

GOSHEN PUBLIC LIBRARY
601 SOUTH FIFTH STREET
GOSHEN, IN 46526-3994

DEMCO